Copy:

MW01533214

ISBN-13: 9798843862749

Cover design by: Anthony R. Case
Library of Congress Control Number: 2018675309
Printed in the United States of America

ANTHONY R. CASE

The Empath and the ~~NARCISSIST~~:
A ~~Love~~ Story

How to Cope, Move on, and Grow as a Person

TABLE OF CONTENTS

CHAPTER 1:

Introduction

I would like to begin by saying do not worry. You will get over your previous partner, and I hope this book helps with that. Herein I will sprinkle past excerpts of real email conversations I had during my narcissistic relationship, and I will then point out my true motivations at the time and how confusing the answers were from the narcissist.

First, a little about me. I am not a licensed therapist or counselor. The opinions contained in this book are my own, and as valid as I believe them to be, that does not make the narcissism of the individual in question a certainty. Be very careful with your own diagnosis. You may feel the need to broadcast it to the world once you finally realize why this person behaved this way. It probably even helped you gain closure, but unless the person in question is diagnosed by a legitimate mental health professional, your opinion is only that. Your opinion. It is dangerous and is most likely best kept to yourself. Narcissism is very difficult to "prove," and since they can never admit that they're wrong, they will fight tooth and nail if you stand up to them in any way. Tread carefully.

However wronged you feel, you must take a step back and travel the high road in this situation. Calling the narcissist out will do no good and is likely to lose you friendships and possibly even land you in court. I have personal experience with this.

Probably very much like you, I am a highly empathic individual who is firmly rooted in reality, believes in truth, and is skilled in conflict resolution. These are a few of the reasons my narcissist chose me. They seek out individuals with these qualities because they know that they themselves are not capable of such things, while also desiring the ability to be empathic like we are. They then study us in order to be able to better imitate empathy because they think that's how everyone else does it. To them, it is not a natural state of mind, but a learned behavior.

They want what they cannot have and take notice when you fail to call them out on their bad behavior as immediately as others have in the past.

This emboldens them. They now consider you a worthy target for a relationship, as you've passed their first test.

In the early days, this will be the best relationship you have ever been in. You'll be amazed at how receptive and likable your new partner is. The phrase "soul mates" may even escape your lips. However, as I learned, just as you may have, old adages have grown old for a reason. As such, if something seems too good to be true, it probably is.

I picked up on it early and even told my partner a few months in that she did not emote like a normal person. I found a few articles that outlined what I had seen so far of her personality and sent them. The result was dead silence.

That is, until she decided to tell me that she "didn't appreciate" me sending her an article about dating a "heartless girl."

I tried to explain that it was a personality

type and not an insult, and that she exhibited all the behaviors mentioned in the article and that I'd like to work with her on it.

Dear reader, this was the first red flag. I was unaware of their existence at the time, and sailed right past many a foreboding crimson marker. In retrospect, if someone reacts to a request for introspection with anger or defensiveness after you've earnestly tried your best to help them, that is a sure sign that you should perform an about face and never look back. This person cannot be helped.

This brings me to my first email excerpt. As this book continues, I'll interject them where relevant, and use them as an example of my mistakes in dealing with a narcissist.

This first one is a few days after I had sent the "Heartless Girl" article. I have edited this excerpt and all others for clarity and anonymity.

> *"Hey!*
>
> *This email isn't going to be as ominous as the title makes it sound . . .*
> *Since I have about twenty minutes before I have to leave, and since I best communicate my thoughts in writing, It seemed like a good idea to*

write you an email and let you know the things we talked about the other evening did not go unnoticed or unacknowledged by me.

Communication is the key to any relationship, and I thought ours was great. At least, I thought I did, but I had over assessed the situation. I knew, for instance, that you'd warned me before about "too much face petting," and I'd altered that behavior, but I didn't realize that meant you didn't like your face touched at all until you said so the other night. I'm glad to know that now. Personal boundaries are incredibly important and we should be able to trust each other at least inasmuch as you know I'm not going to up and touch your face or anything else if you hate it.

Similarly, I'll say this about our relationship - it's wholly unlike any that I've had before it. That's a little scary, but isn't that part of the point? We don't want to be repeating the mistakes of the past, so I see this sort of trailblazing as a good thing. I've really enjoyed getting to know you. Seeing your face light up when something makes you happy is one of the great joys in my life right now. I think, however, that we've been so busy enjoying each other's company and making each other laugh that we've sort of forgotten some other, more complex relationship duties.

Am I storybook head-over-heels in love with you? Probably not. That's a little creepy anyway.

Am I totally infatuated with you and enjoying learning everything I can about you to make myself a better partner? One hundred percent. I don't think I'm ever going to experience "young" love again. I think that with age the sort of recklessness required for that is just no longer in me. Those hormones grew up and started worrying about taxes and retirement savings long ago. When I say I love you, it's just me being excited because I see so much potential in our relationship and that gets me stoked because given my past experience, what's happening here seems to me like it could really work.

That's also not to say that I want to put any pressure on you at all when I say it, but it is going to slip out of me every now and again.

Just give me time to get to know what compromises I need to make, and open yourself up to some you might want to make for me, and then let's talk about them. Communication!

If not, that's also completely understandable, but maybe before any drastic action maybe we go to couples therapy? I feel like although this relationship is young, I'd be more than willing to give it that kind of shot. I think it's worth it."

There is quite a lot to unpack here. This was fairly early on in our relationship - approximately five months in. We had a conversation the day before wherein she complained about me petting her face whenever I kissed her. I should note that I am a hopeless romantic, and at this point I thought I'd found the love of my life, so I enjoyed cradling her face with my hand before a deep kiss.

She, as it turns out, did not like that, and that sparked a one-way conversation about her needs and wants in the relationship.

I didn't know it yet, but I have ADHD, and as such, have always been able to articulate my thoughts more clearly in writing than in person. Everyone else in my life has always found this to be an ideal way to communicate since it allows me time to align my thoughts into an orderly and presentable product. I had never dated anyone who got angry or annoyed at my written communication before, particularly when I was only trying to help.

That specific subject is going to be a bumpy ride as this book continues. No matter how hard I tried, I could not get through to this woman.

So, back to the email. Can you feel how carefully I chose my words here? How I was minimizing my love in order to make it palatable for her? I was already walking on eggshells around her, verbally tiptoeing to avoid an outburst. I thought these were quirks of her personality - negative ones to be sure, but she was so amazing in so many other ways, I let the bad behavior slide, held my nose, and jumped feet-first into what I thought was a relationship that would surely lead to marriage.

I remember speaking to some of my friends just after I sent this email because I thought it was an amusing anecdote from the perspective of a hetero relationship - here was the man begging the woman to talk about her feelings for once.

As with the previous example, I should have seen her stubbornness and unrealistic expectations for what they were. I did not. If I had, this book would be much shorter.

If someone is unwilling to talk about the things that I brought up in this email such as compromise, communication, or couples therapy, pay attention to that. If they are unable to admit any fault in themselves, that is a major red flag.

I could already tell she was unwilling to compromise on anything, and I was beginning to sense that she needed an ego death badly. I would spend the next two and a half years trying to convince her of these things.

For about sixteen months of that, however, she continued doting on me and proving to be a stellar relationship partner. I could hardly believe my luck because she appeared to be as caring as she was beautiful. You will see that I slowly stopped calling her bad behavior out altogether in an effort to keep the peace.

This only prolonged the inevitable.

CHAPTER 2:

Charm?

I myself have often been described as a charming individual. Charm in itself is not a red flag, but it can be a warning sign. In my case, I developed it to thwart bullies as an adolescent. I discovered that if you could make them laugh, they had much less interest in punching you in the face.

This did not stunt my growth into adulthood. It likely created other problems in my young life, but I had no choice but to deal with them. That is all part of growing up.

I remember being at a high school party - there was a girl there that I liked, one thing led to another and we started kissing. I enjoyed this very much, but her parents had to come pick her up, so she left the party. I was still there and after an hour or so began hitting on another nearby girl who I found attractive. She, rightly so, called me out and said something along the lines of "You're not interested in me. You're just interested in sex."

In the moment, I, of course, tried to convince her that was not the case, but looking back, it most certainly was. I was still a kid and hadn't yet developed the emotional maturity to realize how my behavior had made her feel, and that's unfortunate but okay. I'm sure she got over it, and it was a hurtful but necessary lesson, likely for both parties.

I was just a teenager. At that point in life, there is no greater driving force than hormones.

I ruminated on what she said, however. Some time passed, and through introspection, I realized that what I had done that night had been wrong and that I had better correct that behavior quickly or I would never be able to find a genuine partner.

I saw a problem within myself and addressed it. The crux of narcissism is that these people never progressed past this stage. They, through some misguided childhood choice, decided it was better to avoid the pain of real relationships with others than to be hurt again. This, unfortunately, usually originates from a bad family situation. Abusive parents and relatives are a big cause. Clergy or unfortunately, sometimes teachers are another.

At some point during their childhood, an adult betrayed them in some horrible way that caused them to shut down emotionally.

Forever.

As such, I've found that the easiest way to understand why a narcissist acts the way they do is to remember this: Emotionally, they are still children. They may inhabit an adult body and have a successful career, own a home, and even have friends, but their emotional relationship with another person can never develop past surface level. That is why especially covert narcissists, one of whom is the subject of this book, make great friends. However when it comes to a romantic relationship, they are just like the other types and are simply not capable of a deep, meaningful connection with another human being.

Again, charm in itself is not a bad characteristic. I developed it and found it handy in my own life, like when introducing myself to a client. So does the narcissist, but they developed it purely as a defense mechanism and use it to deflect so that they won't have to feel real feelings.

This is why the charm of the narcissist is

difficult to resist at first. To you, the unpracticed empath, you cannot even imagine someone using charm illicitly. You probably won't notice when the narcissist plays off of your personality, mirroring your wants and needs to hook you. It's almost impossible not to fall in love with them because they present themselves as the perfect partner, the one you've been waiting for. They'll cater to your every wanton need.

This soon fades, however, and in fact it has a name: love bombing.

Pay attention to the little things. Do they often seem distant with a vacant look in their eyes? When you go out with them, do they stop paying attention to you, seemingly scanning the room for other potential partners or simply something else to do?

Do they use odd turns of phrase such as I encountered - her favorite was, " . . . because I might be a senator's wife someday." She would use this any time I asked her about being so cold and distant. I remember thinking to myself, *what about being MY wife someday?*

Other sayings may include, "I don't *need* a partner," "If you really loved me, you would/wouldn't have done X," and "Your feelings are valid."

That last one is a masterful move because it makes it seem like they're being understanding.

They are not.

This brings me to my next point.

CHAPTER 3:

*Manipulation, Gaslighting,
and Projection*

*"I've been aware of all the signals for a long
time - your best friend hinting that I should look for
a place nearby, you saying stuff like your neighbors
just "know how you are with guys." There's
nothing wrong with having previous unsuccessful
relationships at all, so I tried to ignore my instincts
and doggedly proceed because I thought that maybe
I could be the one that finally succeeded with you.
But when I would raise my concerns about such
things, you told me there was nothing to worry
about.*

*I'm sorry that I was pushy about some things
and I'm sorry because I kind of feel like I forced you
to come to that music festival and that you really
didn't enjoy yourself. That's on me, but I looked
at it as a learning process for both myself (don't*

act selfish) and you (great, now I know a little more about how she'd like to be treated) and with enough of those, perhaps our relationship could blossom. I'm sorry if I pushed too hard for moving in together. It wasn't my intent to move in and take over your house. In fact, I like your house the way it is, so I thought besides moving in my clothes and putting a TV in the basement, it would have been ideal for both of us.

I ask you, what do you expect out of a relationship that this one isn't providing? It's very strange to me because I know that we will be separating soon because you don't love me nor do you see a future together. I can't force love upon you, nor would I want to if I could, but the strange part is otherwise it feels like absolutely nothing is wrong.

Do you not enjoy my company?

Do we not have fun together in almost any situation?

Do I fail to provide some sort of necessary emotional support?

Sure, there were/are communication issues that need addressing, but I thought we could work those out. That's a relatively small hill to climb.

It just keeps coming around to, at least

from my vantage point, that you never let me in. You never opened yourself up completely to this relationship, and that's the part that really disappoints me.

I'm not sure what your ideal definition of a relationship is, but I do hope you can attain it. However, I hope you're not waiting for perfection, because it's not out there. I honestly thought this one was as close as I was ever going to get."

This email was only two months after the previous one. Reading it, it sounds as if we're already broken up, doesn't it? In fact, I was on the verge of doing so, but I allowed her to manipulate me into staying by assuaging but never really addressing my issues.

This is deflection. They do it so you'll drop the issue and they can continue extracting narcissistic supply from you.

In fact, do you know what she started to call these emails and other communication whenever I broached the subject of her unwillingness to communicate and get close?

"Manipulative."

You, like me, are probably a very genuine person. You can probably feel the conflict I had within me when writing the previous excerpt. I could sense something was wrong and was on the verge of ending the relationship, but with a wave of her hand and a bat of her eyelashes, she convinced me to stay. And after all, in every other regard she'd been the most amazing partner I'd ever had, right? What did I have to lose?

This was the doorway into true manipulation. The gaslight had met a spark.

During this time, she would often react in ways that didn't make any sense to me. Narcissists will frequently behave in ways that don't seem rational. This is because they cannot admit that they are wrong about anything. That would shatter their fragile ego and send their emotional walls tumbling.

If you disagree with one on even the smallest topic, prepare for resignation. They will berate you with their version of the truth until you just can't stand arguing about it anymore, and throw in the towel.

You cannot "win" with the narcissist. Is there someone in your life who will not listen to reason, no matter how pleasantly packaged? Do you know anyone who will argue until they are blue in the face even when you *know* you're right?

Red flags abound.

I once had a twenty minute argument in the car with this woman about whether it was Dollar Tree or Dollar General that sells all items for only one dollar. I had grown up poor in West Virginia and this was something that I knew with absolute certainty. Dollar Tree sells things for only a buck. (A buck twenty-five at the time of this writing, but back then, it was still only a dollar.)

She continued to insist on the opposite. I was in the passenger seat, and she was driving. I, somewhat perturbed, told her to turn at the next light and to drive to a shopping center that I knew contained a Dollar Tree. I would take her inside and prove this to her once and for all.

You may be able to guess what happened instead. Yes, she grew absolutely furious, told me it didn't matter and that I was being insensitive. She asked why I was even so concerned about such a petty thing and bullishly continued on our previously set course to a friend's party.

But it's not a petty thing, I thought to myself. *It's about truth and being intentionally wrong. Why is she doing this?*

As red-faced and angry as she had just been, the moment we parked on the friend's street, her face flushed, and she put on a very genuine smile as we approached the door.

The dollar store incident was soon forgotten, and in fact, we had a wonderful time at the party. In the case of this particular covert narcissist, she had the same ability I did to entertain and be the life of any party. I thought this made us a match made in heaven. We were the envy of all the other couples we met, and that felt good.

Too good.

What is gaslighting? In a nutshell, it's whenever someone insists that you are wrong so vehemently and for so long that you eventually start to believe them, doubting yourself and your own sanity. The dollar store conversation in the car had been an attempt at that. She was testing me to see if I would stand up for myself or fold.

I didn't exactly fold, but I did let the issue drop for the sake of peace, which is something I continued to do for the entire relationship. Again, if someone is completely unreasonable and won't respond to logic or facts, steer as far away as possible.

Sometimes that's not an option if you have children between you or divided pet ownership. In those cases, the gray rock approach is best. Just don't take the bait. Refuse to engage. They're testing you. Give brief, calm, stoic answers. They will eventually tire of casting in your pond and move to another.

I didn't know it yet, but my untreated ADHD made me extra susceptible to gaslighting. My already hyperactive and static-filled headspace was not used to someone openly and blatantly feeding it falsehoods. In fact, I had learned to trust the reliability of others as a way to cope with my day-to-day forgetfulness. In the past, that had been another way for me to trust, bond, and feel closer to my romantic partners. Most even found it endearing. This one had seen that vulnerability and taken advantage of it.

I did see someone wearing a t-shirt recently that said "Gaslighting is not real. You're just crazy," and I got a legitimate chuckle out of it. A year ago that would not have happened.

Healing takes time.

Below is an excerpt from an email that I sent to some of our mutual friends after she had broken up with me. This is jumping ahead a few years in the relationship, but I've placed it here because it fits the current context.

I still had yet to learn a few lessons and had also had yet to identify her as a narcissist. I was still under her spell and believed her when she told me the breakup was all my fault.

I was starting to come out of it though, as evidenced by the below selection.

> "Firstly, she has emotional walls that would make ancient China jealous. I'm talking walls bigger than our former president dreams about at night. In order to maintain these walls, she cannot allow anything in that may damage them, including the truth. She cannot be wrong or the walls might collapse, so reality be damned, she's going to make up a scenario that will keep them supported."

I simply could not leave it alone until I had figured out why she had ended what had been at one time an absolutely amazing relationship. She wouldn't provide a reason. At first, nothing changed at all between us. We still hung out at her house, had sex, and watched movies. The relationship had been

26

what I had always wanted - best friends who have sex sometimes. Isn't that the goal we are all looking for?

So I continued as if nothing had happened for a month or so, I was still in love with her and that is difficult to shut off.

She weaponized the above phrase in an early test by saying we were *just* best friends who had sex sometimes.

I incredulously responded, "But that is literally the definition of a perfect relationship. It's exactly what everyone is out there looking for, and we've got it."

In return I received only a blank stare and a deflection to another subject.

The gaslighting had been so strong, I believed her when she said I was the sole owner and proprietor of Blame, Inc. and had been the reason the relationship had failed.

Projection.

She also told me I have an anger problem, I am manipulative, a "salesman," am untrustworthy, that I lacked confidence, and that I lied.

This is when I should have called her out on all of these which happen to be her own issues, but heartstrings are strong, and I continued to ignore and enable this behavior because I wanted to keep the peace. I even began introspection to see if any of her claims were true. The investigation took a while, and I'm not saying I'm perfect and have never done anything wrong, but I knew I was none of those things. She had been projecting her own issues onto me.

The reason for this goes back to the same reason they can never be wrong. It's the same root cause. If there was something wrong with them, their self-image, which is as fragile and putrid as a rotten egg, would crack. Were that to happen, an odor would undoubtedly escape, alerting others who may begin chipping away at the shell of the narcissistic individual, eventually revealing them for what they truly are in all their messy, smelly glory.

This must be avoided at all costs, so instead, they genuinely inhabit an alternate reality and will gladly perform the necessary mental gymnastics to arrive at a concocted fantasy about your motivations. The dots must be connected in a way that leaves their hands clean and proves their righteousness. Anything less would equal shame, and that is unacceptable.

Their soul is rotten and constantly on the verge of cracking, and just as the empathic individual supposes authenticity in others, they expect everyone to be as incorrigible as they are.

Hence the projection.

CHAPTER 4:

Criticism, Anger, and Selfishness

Being a person who is capable of reason and self-reflection, you probably find constructive criticism to be helpful. I know I do. I really appreciate it whenever someone can share their point of view with me, opening my eyes to how they operate and how to treat them better - or how to perform better at work, or in that next group project.

This is not the case with the narcissistic individual. They view themselves as perfect. It's part of their armor. If you are perfect, then you are impenetrable and always right. This spares them immediate emotional pain, but also does a great deal of damage to the rest of their lives.

They, however, assuming this, don't notice their personal relationships crumbling around them. That is no fault of theirs, so the other people must be to blame, and they, the island oasis of perfection personified, will bravely soldier on. Someone malleable and worthy will eventually land on their shores, of this they are certain.

This is why they are immune to help and even the most delicately packaged constructive criticism will be met with anger or even outright rage.

Have you tried to call the narcissistic individual in your life out on their bad behavior? What was the result?

Anger usually results when the narcissist doesn't get what they want. This can range from a tiny inconsequential thing, to something like being passed up for a promotion. The reason doesn't really matter to them. To them, all that matters is that they've been wronged, and that simply cannot stand.

Remember, on an emotional level, they are still children, and are not capable of a real connection with someone else, true empathy, or genuine love as a result.

How did you behave when you didn't get what you wanted when you were a child? Did you pout? Throw a tantrum? Give the silent treatment? Cry, yell, or argue to get your way?

Now imagine that kind of behavior but displayed by a fully grown adult. It can be quite scary, and sometimes devastating, causing you to cower and abandon your position entirely in the name of peacekeeping.

This is never the right move. Giving in only reinforces their belief that they are right and they will soon find something else to be angry about.

ANTHONY R. CASE

Selfishness comes in many forms from the narcissist. It might not necessarily come in the form of rudeness, line-cutting, and a general lack of self-awareness. Sometimes, especially if young children are involved, it can manifest itself in horrible ways, such as the narcissist preparing their own dinner and eating in front of their hungry children, never to lift a finger for them.

Sometimes the situations can be more complex, such as in the following example, where my girlfriend simply could not grasp that at that moment, my job was more important than an extra ninety minutes with her family.

We were once on a road trip to New England for a wedding. We had been together for probably six months at that point, and it was going to be my first time meeting her wealthy family, who, on a side note, all appear to be well-adjusted and extremely nice people.

At the time, I worked in medical IT. I rarely had to work during "off" hours whenever I wasn't traveling for business, but something came up for a client, and it was my responsibility to fix it before the weekend started. This was for a live hospital environment, after all. They needed their systems running.

We were in my car, driving up the turnpike, whenever the alert came through on my phone, which was doubling as a navigation device but didn't have a strong enough signal to share with my computer. I informed her that I was going to need to find a stable internet connection, and that we were going to have to pull over until I fixed the problem.

She began complaining that we would be late. It was Friday evening, and the wedding wasn't until Sunday morning. I could understand her being anxious to see her family, so I tried to explain to her that it wouldn't take long provided I could find a good internet connection.

So we pulled over at a turnpike rest stop to get gas. I checked their free wi-fi, but I could not get a stable enough signal to establish a secure VPN connection for my work. We got back in the car and drove for about thirty more minutes until I saw a sign for another, larger rest stop. I hoped this one would offer better internet. I flipped on my turn signal and got into the turn lane.

She asked me what I was doing. I explained that this had to be done. It was my job, multiple people were depending on me making this happen, and time was of the essence. It simply was not optional.

She began complaining again about how we would be late. I reassured her that I would be as quick as possible. She was unhappy about it, but relented once she realized I was not going to give her a choice.

I parked the car and she went inside. She did get me a drink and a snack, which was nice, and I found a place outside sitting on a retaining wall that had good enough wi-fi for me to connect.

It was a slow connection, though, so everything I needed to do took longer than normal. After twenty minutes, she began hovering around me, pacing back and forth, and asking me if I was almost finished. I explained the situation, and then she began to lay into me.

Why hadn't I planned for this? What kind of job requires this kind of dedication? Why hadn't I taken the day as a vacation day so we could get there earlier? Was I doing this on purpose to delay us?

I ignored all of her questions until I finally finished my task, and the hospital systems would be back up and running for the weekend. We loaded back in the car, and the tension was palpable. I drove and sipped on my drink and turned on some music.

The music played for a few minutes until she turned it off, and laid into me again with the questions. I was flabbergasted. I thought surely she could understand the urgent nature of my job and how many people were relying on me, but no.

Her primary concern was that we would now be an hour and a half later than originally planned to her parents' lake house. I couldn't believe it.

"Is there some kind of wedding-related event happening tonight?" I asked. Her answer was no.

"Is there going to be a hot meal ready and waiting for us at a particular time?" Again, the answer was no.

"Then we will get there when we get there. It can't be changed. Why are you so upset?"

This is one of the questions that should never be put to the narcissist. The response will range from bluster to outright anger, but will never be constructive or positive in any way.

In this case, she simply stammered for a bit, emitted some kind of nonsensical word salad, and then pouted in the passenger seat for another two hours until we reached our destination.

The moment we pulled in, we were guided to a premium parking spot on the old tennis court, and she jumped out of the car without grabbing any bags and ran inside. This didn't bother me. She was excited to be home. That was fine with me, so

I gathered up all of our luggage and came inside to meet her family.

The rest of the weekend went swimmingly. We had a wonderful time. Her family was lovely and the wedding was a ton of fun and very memorable. I thought we had a deepening bond. Despite her odd behavior, I was still falling more in love with her every day.

After all, she was beautiful, fun, witty, and extremely intelligent - and everyone has flaws. We could work on those.

Couldn't we?

CHAPTER 5:

Inflexibility

This brings us to inflexibility. It falls hand in hand with selfishness. The narcissist cannot relate to other people in a meaningful way. They are too trapped inside their own head to venture out and practice true empathy. They are capable of what's called intellectual empathy, which is a function of real empathy, but without the ability to imagine themselves in the place of another individual. Instead, they can rely only on learned reactions to events that they have found usually works favorably.

During a discussion after our breakup, mine actually sent me a meme asking me to be more empathetic toward her needs. I could not seriously believe she was asking for this. Was she not aware that I had been bending over backwards for her for three years to keep her happy and to keep her from blowing up and getting angry at the drop of a hat?

How could I possibly have been more empathetic than that?

I realized that when I looked around her house, it was a somber memorial of the handiwork of boyfriends past. One had been an electrician and had rewired the place. One had left a set of tools in the basement with his name scribed on them.

It felt strange as I used those same tools to repair some windows, fix an upside-down light switch, level a door, and install a large custom stained glass window I gave her one Christmas, all the while I believing that I would be different - the one that could win her over.

I helped her carry a broken washing machine out from her basement, where it had been sitting, I presume, since the last boyfriend had refused to remove it.

None of this had meant anything to her. One of my primary love languages is Acts of Service, if you hadn't already guessed. These events were meaningful to me as it seemed like we were building a life together.

However, now I'm sure she tells the same stories to new boyfriends as she told to me - every one of her past relationships ended badly and she has had bad luck with dating guys who turned out to be real jerks in the end. The last one was so bad she accused him of stalking and changed her locks!

✓ This is another red flag. If all of their previous relationships ended badly and they can't accept responsibility for at least some of the blame, get out.

It was also around this time that I started to realize that she had never catered to any of my needs at all. Not a single one. Just before she broke up with me, I had lost my job of ten years. That was a devastating blow that I thought she could relate to since just a year before, she had gone through a similar situation with a tough boss at work, coming home almost every night complaining about it.

This new authority figure allegedly had no idea how they were manipulating people and potentially ruining their lives. The new boss also apparently had it out for my girlfriend and was full-on attacking her, nitpicking and micromanaging to the extreme. She'd been with that organization for years, and suddenly she had this new boss who was making things rough.

I thought to myself, *You know, this sucks right now. She's distraught and there's nothing I can do to help other than to be supportive until it all blows over.*

Then she'll be back to being the amazing woman she usually is.

I was correct, and provided her the necessary support to make her feel better, but when a nearly identical scenario happened to me a year later - even down to a new boss who was suddenly scrutinizing every little thing I did despite the fact that I was a senior engineer and had been with the company for ten years. I was an expert in the field and I had reluctantly signed each write up with a detailed explanation about why I disagreed with it.

By the time the second write up came, I knew what was happening. We had just been bought by a larger company, and this new boss was looking to fire me and set an example.

One may think that during this time, I would have gotten the same support from my girlfriend as I had given her a year prior, no?

What I got instead was asked what I was really doing wrong, and was told that he must have a reason for what he's doing and that I needed to find out the cause and take corrective action immediately. This is all good advice from a professional perspective, but it was not the emotional support I had been looking for.

All I wanted was for her to tell me everything was going to be okay, and to maybe hug me or take me out to a movie or something - *anything* would have helped, but I got nothing but cold, hard business advice.

During this time, she was preparing to start a new job. She'd been driven out of her old one by the new boss, and she'd found a new one in the private sector that paid nearly twice as much. She was going to start earning insane amounts of money, and I told her how proud I was of her for turning that bad situation around.

I, had of course, eventually been fired from my job, and did not rest on my laurels. I filed for unemployment, updated my resume, and began submitting. I was full of hope for the future. She had this great new job lined up, and I would land one soon.

We had been fighting a bit lately, but I knew that could be worked out and was probably due to both of us having been under so much work-related stress.

I was excited for a fresh start together. We

could use this as a springboard into a new life - one that we'd pulled from the ether for ourselves using only sheer will and determination. It seemed like a nice way to leave the past behind. I saw it as poetic.

Instead, two months before I was to start my new job and quite literally moments after I had completed a multi-day, multi-hundreds of miles bicycle tour, still coated in trail dust, sweat, and sunscreen, she asked me to come over to her house. I said that I would like to, but that I was tired and wanted to go home and shower and get a good night's sleep first.

Then she said she wanted me to come over now because she needed to speak to me and it needed to be "in person."

That's right. I was about to be broken up with, and I was a two hour drive away. I had time to think.

This should have been the precipice of a new beginning, an opportunity for us to grow closer and to deepen our bond via triumph over hardship, but it wasn't. The woman who had begged me for more empathy didn't even have the courtesy to wait until I'd showered off the muck before breaking up with me. I was still in my full cycling kit, padded shorts and all, a stinky and sweaty mess.

But I was given no real reasons, and told that I was crazy when I asked for closure.

I simply could not understand how she had not seen things the same way I did. It made no sense until I started learning about narcissists and how they will break up with partners just before a significant life change such as this because they blame all of their problems on their partner, and believe discarding them is their only route to happiness.

Around this same time, a few months before the breakup, due mostly to her criticism, I had decided to get tested for ADHD. I was a forty-one year old man who had been a little behind on all of life's milestones, who, to be sure, had ultimately clawed his way up from poverty into a successful career. I was proud of that.

But I knew something wasn't right.

There were times when she was actively complaining about me not paying attention to her - moments when I desperately *wanted* to pay attention to keep her happy, or rather placated now that I think about it, but I simply couldn't. I'd think, *I know I need to pay attention to her right now. Okay, concentrate . . . Oh look, the clock is off on the microwave. I had better fix that. Oh, it looks like rain outside. I had better let the dog in. While I'm out there . . .*

"What? Yes, of course I'm paying attention."

This should sound familiar to any ADHD sufferers and their partners.

On one hand, she was being quite unreasonable, but on the other she had a point. I was kind of over her constant woe-is-me attitude, but on this one issue however, she was actually on to something. I could not pay attention even when I wanted to.

I saw a psychiatrist, got prescribed medication, and started learning all about ADHD. I was brought to tears as my whole life suddenly began to make sense. My shortcomings were not laziness, but were due to untreated symptoms of a real disorder. I had been behind on all of life's major milestones because the ADHD brain takes extra time to mature.

Another entire book could be written and in fact many already have been about the adult diagnosis of ADHD.

I found the whole process nothing short of revelatory.

I now had the tools to take back control of my own life.

This was going to be a fresh start in more ways than one! Now that I knew about my disorder, I could make an honest effort to pay attention to her. I also explained that I had begun taking medication which takes a month or two to fully take effect, but in the future, I would be so much better about attention-related issues because I was willing to do the work and just being aware of the problem is most of the battle.

Again, I was excited.

But it didn't matter to her. She had already decided I was the source of all of her current problems. I was unceremoniously dumped over a dinner of take-out burrito bowls, then, inexplicably, invited to stay and watch a movie.

I declined and went home.

From there I went reeling into a downward spiral. I had loved this woman with all my heart and had been utterly convinced that we were soulmates.

I wanted to spend the rest of my life with her, and we had in fact discussed that many times over pillow talk.

How could she do this to me? What kind of a person can just shut off a mostly wonderful relationship of three years that had no real problems to speak of other than some communication issues which could easily be worked out?

Then it dawned on me.

In those three years, she had never once uttered those three little words to me. I got told "I saw the *potential* to love you, but I don't."

For all that time, I had been pining for it and waiting for her to say those three words. I told my friends about this issue and insisted that she must but probably just has trouble vocalizing it because who in their right mind would spend almost three years with someone they did not love?

Love is not some commodity to withhold and

use as bait. It's not a bargaining tool with which to pry what you want from someone.

Why had I stayed with this person for so long? I had even tried to end it a few months in because I sensed she was missing something. My gut had sensed the danger and tried to warn me. Why hadn't I gone through with it then?

The answer is that I was an unpracticed empath - a people pleaser, and deftly skilled at it. I had been entirely unaware of red flags and boundaries. I had given and given and given to this woman and received nothing in return. She and all narcissists are a black hole of empathy. You put endless amounts in, but none ever comes back out.

It was time for some more self-work.

CHAPTER 6:

Trust Your Gut

"Hey honey,

I was thinking about what you said the other night and I wanted to let you know about one thing that you're wrong about. My self-confidence.

I have it in spades. I wear what I want, (okay, the shorty shorts were your idea, and a good one at that.) speak my mind when I want, and throughout my whole life, I've been able to win over and influence people.

What I've been unconfident about is this relationship, and for quite some time because I didn't fully understand your point of view. I can see from where you stand that I may have come across a guy who is lacking confidence, because this relationship is the only window you can see me through, but remember when we were first dating and I won you over with said confidence?

Am I unconfident in my own body? Nope. I know what it is and how to keep it going and be the version of me that I WANT TO BE. I absolutely do not expect the same out of you, but please don't mistake my desire to stay fit for a lack of confidence. It's completely the opposite!

In fact, I'm a little vain. You've noticed. I know that's not a great quality. I'm working on it. I'll also do my best not to worry about my body in front of you. Yours is sexy as hell, and I guess mine is too. :)

Also, don't assume that because I'm hard on myself that way that I don't like you the way you are. I wouldn't be here if I didn't. I wouldn't be here at all if I wasn't crazy about you.

Could I find someone else if it doesn't work out with you? Yeah, I have no doubt. I just don't want to. When I first met you, I knew you were the girl I'd been looking for - for ages. I honestly had expected to be single for a few years, because believe it or not, I'm quite picky about my partners, and you came along when I was least expecting it. I was blindsided, but super happy.

I have, however, been super concerned that you don't love me and I'm looking for an eventual wife. You wouldn't want to husband a guy who didn't love you, would you?

. . . I sensed that change in attitude from you, and boom, the confidence I had in winning you over was lost.

What does all this mean?

Well, it means that I'm working on repairing some things . . . my confidence in YOU.

I won't make empty promises. This email is the last I'll talk about it until you bring it up again. I just felt like I should fully explain how I got here for your understanding.
And, I'm finally gonna write it out -

Love,
Anthony"

This was about fifteen months into the relationship. My instincts had been screaming at me to abandon this woman. They couldn't have been more clear, but I swept them under the rug and proceeded anyway.

I had even been through a similar situation a few years before, with someone who wasn't a full-on narcissist, but who definitely was over critical yet hypersensitive to criticism herself. I was recognizing this pattern again. She had also questioned my confidence when in fact, I can border on brash at times.

The similarity here was that I had been able to win over both women with said confidence, but at a year or so in, they began odd critical behavior that undermined the structure of the relationship while gently nudging me away.

After several months of this, I would change my behavior to compensate - walking on eggshells to avoid further conflict/criticism/complaint.

This was a red flag that I had let go twice now.

Then my partner would come with the accusation of lack of confidence, which, in respect to the relationship, was absolutely true given that they had been working steadily at undermining it with criticism and put-downs to which I was not allowed to respond for fear of being called "defensive."

Why had these women who had been so much fun in the early stages in the respective relationships worked so hard to push me away?

It was testing. They were probing to see how much I would put up with. It was as much my problem as it was theirs, because I had yet to learn to establish boundaries and learn that they are enforceable.

It's okay to say no.

It may momentarily break the peace, but if it does, would the resulting dialogue not be worth it? Wouldn't a few minutes of fighting be the confirmation you need that something's wrong, and wouldn't a frank discussion about the issue be progress?

After a year of constant criticism, I had told this previous partner, "I don't know how I managed to make it thirty-seven years on this planet without you hovering over my shoulder to make sure I do everything right."

She laughed and thought it was a joke. It was not. I was really hurt by her behavior and was trying to let her know that.

I warned that her constant negativity and criticism was really turning me off to the point that I wanted to end the relationship. I begged her to work on it. I gave her a timeline of one year to do so, which in retrospect was awfully generous. We had already been together for almost five years at that point though, and I was buying heavily into sunken-cost fallacy.

The year passed, and with no progress or effort from her, true to my word, I let myself into her apartment just after the new year. I did this before she got home from work, and packed all my things.

I waited calmly at the kitchen table for her to get home. I knew that having my things packed was the only way I would go through with it today. I knew that she would try to talk me out of it and I had to be strong.

She came home, said hello, and went to the bedroom. She emerged a few minutes later crying. The jig was up.

My hands were shaking.

I was afraid that she would get angry, but no, she just cried for a while and indeed bargained with me to stay.

I explained that while it was devastatingly painful for me, this had to be done. This relationship had become unhealthy and I simply could not face the prospect of spending another year in it.

Even though I had initiated the breakup,

the aftermath was difficult. I had to resist the temptation to call or text her randomly throughout the day, as I had become so accustomed to doing over the last several years.

As the weeks went on and I gained perspective, I realized what had gone wrong in the relationship and vowed not to let that happen again.

I was single for only two months before the narcissist entered my life.

She seemed at first to be the most amazing creature I'd ever met. It was like we'd known each other our entire lives! Our first date turned into a sleepover, and never stopped from there. I believe I stayed with her for three days on that first date that neither of us wanted to end.

I was flabbergasted. How could this happen so soon? I had fully expected to be single for a while, testing chemistry, striking out, hitting the occasional home run, and unfortunately, breaking a few hearts along the way.

But here was this ravishing woman, full of life and charisma and almost all of the same interests as me! We literally never stopped talking when we were together. Sometimes we wouldn't even need to turn the television on, simply engaged in conversation for hours well past bedtime.

The timing couldn't have been worse, but I reasoned that you just can't put a clock on this type of thing. When you meet a unicorn, well, that's when you meet them and you can't wait around for another one, can you?

Both cautious, but for different reasons, we enacted a customary two-month exclusivity rule. This meant that we could both continue dating others until the two months were up, at which point we'd decide to make it exclusive or not.

I had a few more dates, but who was I kidding? No one's energy and chemistry matched hers. She was the woman I didn't think existed - a twin flame - an actual soul mate.

I immediately fell in love.

However, those few months in, my gut started poking at me. I noticed how she treated people rudely quite a lot of the time, and actually seemed downright cold and calculating in certain interactions with others. I tamped my gut down and told it that those were only "business" transactions, and that surely she wouldn't manipulate me in the same way. I was her one - her true soulmate. We could trust each other implicitly.

Couldn't we?

I am today shocked at my own past naivete.

I'm assuming one of the reasons you picked up this book is because you have reached a similar place in your own personal journey. As an empath, we are both the rarest and most vulnerable personality type. When unguarded, we will gladly allow and even openly invite in untold amounts of damage from loved ones.

Yes, you've got a big heart and a lot of love to give, but you can't let someone take advantage of that. You need to protect yourself by making limits and standing up for your own mental health.

You probably thought you were good at reading people, right? I did. I've always prided myself on being able to accurately assess someone's character almost immediately. Do you know what the number one earliest sign I should have picked up on with my narcissist was?

I couldn't get a read on her. She broke my trusty personality meter.

Most of the time, it's easy to tell malicious people, right? They wear it on their sleeves and don't disguise it at all. It's also very easy to spot narcissists from the outside, correct? They're blustery and loud, and always need to be the center of attention. They are never wrong and often act childish.

But when you're the target of one, especially a covert one, it's almost impossible not to fall for them. They are absolute masters of manipulation. That time that you thought was the two of you getting to know each other in the beginning of the relationship?

That was the narcissist taking inventory and picking apart how you work. The reason they seem like your soulmate is because they've spent the time breaking your personality down, learning how to cater to your needs and desires in order to hook you.

That time they spent breaking down your personality? When was that?

That was during the earliest stages of the relationship while you were distracted by love.

Then they mirror your own personality back at you, creating what you think is an amazing bond, but to them is literally a game, one that they've played before and you haven't.

None of it is actually meaningful, yet they are

able to mimic a loving relationship so well that they lure you closer and closer.

The claws begin sinking in yet you're convinced it's merely a thorny rose.

More recently, I've learned to trust my instincts in situations like this. I'd have avoided a world of pain, but also at the same time, that was a vital lesson learned that I'll never repeat again. I actually appreciate it because I was blindly feeling my way around for a partner, testing for chemistry and nothing else.

Without her and without this lesson, I didn't know what I truly wanted in a relationship and didn't know exactly what I needed in a partner.

Now I do, and that's powerful. Mutual respect is at the top of that list.

I did not do it alone. I found a great therapist who took me in at what was probably the lowest point in my life. I had lost my decade-long job, been dumped by the woman I thought I was going to marry, been diagnosed with ADHD, got a new job, bought a house, and moved for the first time in twelve years - all in a short three month span.

After a single session whenever I explained a lot of the things that my ex-girlfriend said and did to me, she would reply matter-of-factly, explaining what had happened there, and that no, I wasn't imagining things, and that yes, that had been gaslighting. It immediately helped, but therapy isn't instant.

It takes time - to get to know your therapist, but also for you to do the work and to come around to the conclusions on your own. A good therapist only helps you there, leads you to water, so to speak. You've got to take those last steps for yourself, actually bending over to take a drink.

CHAPTER 7:

Hypersensitivity

What sort of image does that word, "hypersensitivity" conjure up in your mind? A cranky child? If it does, you're not too far off the reason for the narcissist's absolute disdain for any sort of criticism whilst happily handing out plenty of it themselves.

Yes, it's a double standard. Do they know that? Maybe. Do they care? Absolutely not, because they are perfect. That means that double standards do not apply to them, because they're *different.*

They consider themselves to be better than everyone else - on a higher plane, even. They have disdain for the emotional person, because they trained themselves long, long ago that emotions were bad and only led to harm, to be avoided at all costs.

It plays nicely into the old sci-fi trope of the emotionless android. They can function as a high-ranking officer on their vessel, carrying out important duties, are dependable, and have the full trust of the captain and the crew. They're treated as an equal crew member with a rank and everything, but eventually, that emotionless android always desires to be human, and how do they go about it?

Well, usually, their efforts begin with an attempt to seduce a fellow crew member, normally to comedic effect.

It is exactly the same with the narcissist, except no one's laughing.

The narcissist sees themselves in much the same way. Since they consider emotion inferior, they tend to regard themselves as a machine of sorts. They require maintenance and upkeep (food, exercise, etc.) just like the sci-fi android. They tend to look at these metrics in black and white and know that's simply what's necessary to perform their best. They can also be extremely successful and acquire wealth, which further bolsters their image of self-perfection while worsening the problem.

And also like our android friend, they are

absolutely abysmal at interpersonal relationships. Sure, they've learned how to act and even emulate others through trial and error, perfecting their sexual techniques or responses to the emotional needs of others in order to *appear* human, but rest assured, they are not. Not fully, anyway. Just like our android crew member, they are incapable of empathy. They can't completely understand the human condition without it, but they keep trying, because everyone else seems so good at it.

But remember, the narcissist cannot escape their own head.

They truly view every other person in the world as an extension of themselves.

They think we are all built and operate the same way. It's the only way they know, so they assume everyone else must be the same. This leads them to write a script in their head with your part in it. A program, if you will. Deviation from that script will equal hell to pay. As long as you play your part, though, there will be harmony, but remember, it's all still an emotionless act. They don't *really* have a connection with you or love you.

To complete the metaphor, just like our sci-fi android officer, they may look, sound, speak, move, and be fully anatomically functional - by all accounts appearing to be human, but they are not.

The real difference being, the sci-fi character always recognizes this as a limitation and wants to become "a real boy," to mix metaphors a bit.

The narcissist is unable to recognize that they're missing something, that they're not a complete human. Unlike the android, they are not capable of introspection. They believe themselves perfect as is, and the reason everyone else seems to be put off by them is because they've never met anyone who is truly perfect before.

That's not their fault. It's yours. *flipped*

why can't that switch be flipped back on?!?!

How does all this lead to hypersensitivity? You may have already guessed. They are used to their actual loved ones, family, mostly, kowtowing to their every mood. They've collectively been walking on eggshells for years, decades even, and it's all they know. It's their normal.

I was with my narcissist and her mother one time. The narc was complaining about having difficulty losing weight, and pointing out how seemingly easy it is for her older sister to stay in shape.

Her mother said, "I don't know honey, it just must be something genetic with you."

Do you know how badly I wanted to cue the record scratch sound effect? The *what* now? They're biological sisters aren't they? Same mother, same father? No one else in the family has a weight problem, and you're blaming her overeating on *genetics*?

I realize weight can be a sensitive topic, but when asked outright, even her own mother was so used to avoiding conflict with her hypersensitive daughter that she made up a reason just to satiate her temper and avoid a fight.

nothing I do will ever be enough

Never mind that her sister, like myself, works out constantly, watches her diet and probably like myself, keeps track of her dietary needs in order to stay fit while her narcissistic younger sister runs a 5k every once in a while, but can otherwise be found on the couch.

The narcissist even said to me one day that her sister has complained that her hands go numb whenever she exercises hard enough, and why would someone want to do that to their body?

I replied with, "You know, that happens to my hands quite often on long bike rides. You've got to shake them out and get the blood flow back in them and . . ."

"You must hate your body then, to put yourself through that."

"What? No, it's exactly the opposite, We're only here once, and we only get one body. I want to take care of mine and make sure it lasts as long as possible."

That did not compute, so she disengaged the conversation.

They cannot comprehend alternate points of view.

On the other side of the hypersensitivity coin is their willingness to criticize you, their lover. They will have absolutely no problem with pointing out every little thing they perceive as a flaw in you, who unlike them, are not perfect.

What's more, since they aren't capable of introspection, self-care, and change, they assume you aren't either and that any flaws present therein are permanent.

You've now been labeled defective by the narcissist. If you upset them any more by calling out their bad behavior, or by deviating from their pre-written script they have for you, they will begin looking for an opportunity to discard you.

After all, they can't have a defective biological being as their partner. They need another who is as perfect as they are.

If they don't match with another narcissist, the only other possible match for one is a total "yes" person, who like we were at one point, most likely begins as an unpracticed empath. They probably mean well, and see the shiny, attractive, charismatic, successful narcissist as a beacon, so they shrink their own needs down to obey the narc's every desire, basking in the warm glow of the narc's attention and becoming a master eggshell walker and trusted ally - after all, they will never, ever say "no" to the narcissist and injure their fragile ego.

They will always stay on-script, never to disappoint.

the constant
talking w/ gurls!
UGH!!!! VERY disappoint
ing! I try to keep his
interest, I will never be
enough :')

CHAPTER 8:

Minimization and Loss

By now we've reached a point at or near the end of the relationship. Your narc has decided that you are a defective emotional being and your genuineness enrages them. They can't stand to look at you any longer. Where you still see the person that you fell in love with and with whom you still hope to work things out, they see an enemy.

You've gone too far off script and they are at risk of being exposed and they know it. You dared to think for yourself and now you're going to pay the price for it.

It may seem to come out of left field - a complete surprise, but look back. There were warning signs.

You had your rose colored glasses on, and

when you're wearing those, all the red flags just look like flags.

Now you'll experience the true depths and coldness of the relationship that you thought was there. It was all an illusion, an unwanted and expertly performed trick.

To them, it was a way to see how long they could keep you hooked without thinking for yourself. They never loved you. A narcissist can't love in the traditional sense. They only love your source of narcissistic supply, not you as an individual person.

Another story comes to mind. We had gone to Florida to visit her family's winter home, and the narcissist's best friend came along. In retrospect, this seems strange, but at the time it was not. It was completely normal. It was almost as if I was dating the two of them sometimes. Her best friend was platonic and the only person who was allowed inside her walls because she had mastered the delicate balance of eggshell walking, pettiness, and compliance that it takes to get truly close to a narc.

At any rate, we had a pretty lovely trip with one exception. On one of the nights, her friend and her parents had gone to bed early, so we agreed on a romantic late-night rendezvous in the pool.

She went to change into her bathing suit, and I proceeded to the bathroom, letting her know I was going to go ahead and get ready for bed - my usual routine of toothbrushing, contact lens removal, moisturizing, et cetera.

After probably five minutes, I was finished, changed into some swim trunks, and excitedly went out to the pool to meet her. The lighting was dim and romantic, but she was sitting on the edge, feet in the water, and was angry.

I asked why and she said that she thought that I had abandoned her and gone to bed, leaving her out here all alone. I explained that of course that was not the case and that I had told her I was going to get ready for bed before joining her. It had only been a few minutes, I told her, and I do the same bedtime routine every night. She knows how long it takes.

This seemed like a reasonable time saving measure to me. This way when we were finished with our swim, she could have the single bathroom all to herself to prepare for bed. I did not see a problem at all. In fact, I had been anticipating her needs, and now she was angry about it.

She would not be convinced, however, and told me that I'd ruined the mood, extracted her feet from the pool, and marched to the bedroom.

I was left yet again trying to figure out what had happened and what kind of story she'd made up in her head to make me the bad guy in this situation.

I followed her into the bedroom after a few minutes, giving her time to cool down. She grumbled something about me being inconsiderate, rolled over, and turned off the light.

Narcissists truly believe that the world is out to get them. They have a persecution complex because they believe everyone else is jealous of their perfection. This was not the first nor the last time she would attribute malice to my actions when my intent was pure.

The trip home was eventful as well. I was treated to a new kind of selfishness. I was still working a travel job at the time, and I had more airline miles to my name than I knew what to do with, so I flew all of us first class for free.

The girls were giddy. Neither had ever flown in first class before. They began drinking, learned that drinks were free in first class, and then they drank some more whilst also chatting very loudly and collecting side-eye from other passengers. This was a bit embarrassing for me, as this is not how one should behave in first class, but they were having fun and I let it go without saying anything.

That is, until we landed and it was clear that my girlfriend was too drunk to drive safely. I voiced my concerns. I had been pulled over for a DWI a few years prior, something that I wasn't and still am not proud of. That experience had drilled into me the dangers of drunk driving and I refused to get in the car if she was behind the wheel.

I was sober and offered to drive, but she got angry and refused to give me the keys. I pleaded passionately for her to let me drive all of us home, but her mind was made up and she was going to drive.

We got to the car, started loading luggage into it, and suddenly she couldn't find her phone, which doubled as her wallet. This equaled a huge fight in public wherein I offered that if I can't drive, then we should all just combine our efforts to find the phone, then take the train back home and return tomorrow for the car.

She grew furious and told me to fuck off. She was being so unreasonable that I was perfectly inclined to do so, so I began walking toward the train platform. However I realized that in the commotion, my keys had been left behind in her car so I couldn't go home just yet.

Meanwhile, the two of them had gone to retrace their steps in the airport to look for the phone. I returned to the car to find the back hatch hanging full sail open, with all of our bags on public display.

I counted us lucky that no one had helped themselves to our belongings in the ten or so minutes I'd been gone, and began digging my backpack out from amongst the other luggage when suddenly I saw it.

She had set the phone down on top of a suitcase, then loaded a few others on top, and instead of looking around, she panicked and assumed she had left it on the aircraft. The car keys were also there, next to the phone.

Thank goodness she left the car open, it turned out, but now I was seriously conflicted. I could close the hatch and walk away, but if I did that, she might be searching fruitlessly in the airport for hours, and then would not be able to get into her car and unable to call for help. I also knew there would be hell to pay if she found out I had done that intentionally. I could just drive the car home and wait for them to eventually tire and take the train back, but that also did not seem like a good option. I couldn't convince myself that my girlfriend wouldn't report her car stolen if I tried that. I did not have any contact information for her friend either. She never trusts any of her best friend's boyfriends for some reason.

I decided that the best and least petty thing to do was to grab my bag and her keys, leaving everything else locked safely in the car. Then I would literally run down the hallway toward the terminal in an attempt to catch them.

They were retracing their steps and moving slowly, and I soon caught sight of them.

As I neared, I said, "I was going to fuck off as instructed, but then I found the keys in the back of the car, which was hanging wide open. Also, your phone is not lost. It was there too. Here it is, and here are your keys. Goodbye."

As I turned to leave she did something unexpected.

She thanked me.

This sucked me back in. It was such a rare event that it felt extra rewarding - like a gold star in elementary school, that apology meant more to me than it should have. I was somehow talked into riding with them, with my girlfriend driving. I think she had convinced me that losing her phone had sobered her up enough. Either that or I just relented because I was so tired of all the arguing, something that had become alarmingly frequent.

I don't remember which, but I do remember that car ride home was utterly hair-raising and I absolutely should not have let her drive. I white-knuckled the backseat handle the entire way. Luckily, we got to her house safely, had dinner and soon forgot about the incident.

Under the rug it went, never to be discussed again.

She minimized how inebriated she was in order to make an excuse for driving. She was also unable to admit that she was too drunk, or that would burst her personal bubble of perfection. The whole thing had been an exercise in the minimization of the feelings of not just me, but the lives of everyone else on the road including myself and her best friend.

Minimization is also another component that explains how they can be so cold and calculating. Narcissists prevail in high-level business positions where tough decisions are the norm. They have no problem with administering discipline or firing. It's also why they can be so cold to you, their partner. However, if they themselves are disciplined at work or in any other way, prepare for an onslaught of relentless self-pity. The person who administered that discipline is a manipulative, lying, cheating, control freak who has to exert their power over others in order to feel good about themselves.

Does that sound familiar?

Have you ever described your narcissistic relationship as "hot and cold?"

This is the reason why. The narc can only be "loving" and "love" when they have something to gain, and when they are nice, it's as if niceness itself descended from the heavens upon you. There is that superficial charm working again. They know precisely how to butter you up to gain your compliance and they're not shy about doing it.

Conversely, when they have nothing to gain, you're merely an inconvenience - something to be avoided like a pothole in the road or a bad restaurant. Not like a living, breathing, empathic human being, but like an inanimate object. You're useless to them if you're not providing narcissistic supply in the form of praise, service, or sex.

Outburst are never talked about. Its very frustrating that I can't talk to him about feelings.

Speaking of sex, it will be used as a weapon against you. One minute they will be catering to your every sexual desire, the next, they will refuse to even touch you.

At about two years into the relationship, she insulted the size of my penis. This was during the throes of intercourse one night, and we were not sober. I didn't know if it was some kind of joke or an attempt at teasing, but I did know that I had nothing to worry about. All I could do was laugh it off because I knew it wasn't true.

What it was was another attempt at control and poking at my boundaries. If I had responded favorably and agreed with a literal insult to my manhood, then she would know I would acquiesce to anything. It was another test, and by standing up for myself, I had failed.

She had begun to push my nearly infinite supply of patience too far. These failed tests began lining up like dominos.

She had said to me once that she knew that she occasionally failed to do the right thing or follow good advice even when she knew it would be good for her.

I responded that was because she didn't know

how to compromise and always had to do things her way. I reminded her she'd said in her online dating profile that she was "looking for a relationship that lasts longer than a tube of toothpaste."

For almost three years, I had been playfully holding up each new tube of toothpaste every time we started one and teasing her about it. One day she got extremely angry and bitterly told me not to remind her of anything she said in her dating profile.

I posited that these two things were likely related and that she needed to learn how to compromise and reiterated that we are all just individual people in the world who are trying our best to get by and no one is perfect.

She began talking about breaking up and said that she would wait until COVID was over before making a final decision. This was sometime in 2021.

Not long thereafter, she told me I was mistreating her, but when I asked for examples, she would only mention household chores like "You don't take the trash out when you say you are going to." This apparently equated to "broken promises," something which I took very seriously since I believe in truth and keeping my promises above almost anything else.

My sincere approach and desire to solve the problem seemed to annoy her further.

I explained that I did always eventually get the trash out, but I would get distracted along the way by any number of things that might need attention like putting dishes away, folding laundry, or fixing something around the house before making it outside to the trash cans.

I failed to see how actually performing *more* chores than promised equaled both a broken promise and mistreatment.

Next I was told that it was because I never asked questions about her or her family. I explained how that felt pre-diagnosis in an email after the breakup:

"I agree that you deserve someone who is interested in your life and asks you questions. I wasn't doing that, but that doesn't mean that I didn't care about your life or was uninterested. Of course both are true. I was simply unable to find a way through all the static to express those things to you - thoughts unable to be spoken. They seemed . . . inexpressible, ethereal, possibly witches' magic."

I don't ask because I don't know if it will be one of his stories.

The truth of the situation had been that she never asked about *my* needs or family, and we had enjoyed each other's company so much and indeed already knew everything about each other's families, so that it did not seem like an urgent, relationship-ending issue to me. I explained that if asking personal questions and being expedient with the trash were important to her, that I would be happy to do those things, and she told me it was too little too late.

She was, in fact, simply throwing reasons against the wall in hopes that one would stick and I would be satisfied. In reality, I had caught on to and stopped playing her games, halting her narcissistic supply. That is truly the reason why she wanted to break up. It does not matter how hard you try. Nothing you do will ever be good enough for them if you are no longer a source of supply.

Toward the end, a few months later, she began physically recoiling when I attempted to kiss her. It was so bizarre, I could not make sense of it. Who could be so childish? I thought surely that wasn't the answer. This went on for a few months. I had longish hair at the time and she said it was because the fine hairs out front would tickle her forehead and cause an involuntary reaction.

She really said that and I actually believed her, given that the alternative was just as absurd and I didn't want it to be true. In actuality, of course, she was shutting down. She'd labeled the relationship as over and deemed me to no longer be a viable partner.

She had to convince herself that I was a bad person in order to internally justify the breakup.

She had also begun the devaluation of me as a person, and in a lot of ways, that can hurt the most. Now you are not only no longer a love interest, you're actually a contemptible person from whom they cannot wait to distance themselves. The insults will take wings and fly.

How did this happen? How could I go from the person with whom she'd discussed donating her body together with to science - to one of those museum exhibits - with the stipulation that they be posed with our hands clasped so that we could literally hold hands forever.

How could it possibly go from that to this?

I had yet to solve the riddle, but I now knew without a doubt that something was seriously wrong with this woman. We were inseparable best friends. We finished each other's sentences and had a hundred inside jokes. We had enjoyed nearly every activity that two consenting adults could possibly enjoy together. It had been, despite the occasional bouts of doubt and turmoil, the best relationship I had ever been in.

And now it was the worst.

I had yet to educate myself on narcissism nor had I noticed the patterns of lies and manipulation. As I stated earlier, I had assumed that all of her odd behavior was simply due to a few negative personality traits and that the woman behind those traits was still worthy of my love.

When the hot ran hot, it was scalding and we were absolutely perfect together. However, I had begun to gray rock and not respond to her tests and insults. I would instead take a breath, collect my thoughts, and reply stoically and void of emotion.

The final domino was placed.

"Hey,

Happy Tuesday and second day of your new job to you! I hope it continues to be good and your new laptop doesn't go into orbit!

I'm sorry I've been peppering you with observations and questions lately. I feel like I just need closure on the whole thing. You keep saying "forward only," and I agree with that, but I just need to go through some things first.

Sometimes I feel totally indifferent because you obviously just weren't in it anymore and it didn't matter how hard I was trying because your mind was made up.

Looking back at the timeline, I emailed you almost precisely one year before I actually went and got treatment for ADHD. I knew it was affecting things then but you discouraged me from looking into a diagnosis, so I didn't. How different could that year have been?

Despite my actions and occasional brash behavior, I really did love you and wanted to fix things.

During that time, my old job was falling apart, and being untreated, I just couldn't deal with the pressure and pretty much shut down. I was a sourpuss all the time because I didn't have the tools in my repertoire to deal with it. I ended up taking a lot of that stress out on you, and I'm really sorry for it. I think that was the major contributor to the break up and it makes me really sad.

Oh well though. Whatifs never do anyone any good, and all I can do from here is improve and be the better person I was trying to be.

I'm going to miss hanging out in your backyard, grilling, and listening to music before having a fire. I'm going to miss aimless walks, whether they be around your neighborhood or in Florida. I'll miss holding your hand and going to the movies. I'll miss camping at the beach. I'll miss those nights when we didn't even need to turn on the TV but could just sit and talk all night. Those were the best, but I guess it turns out we should have been talking about our feelings a little more back then.

I'll stop now because I know you hate these emails."

Let's unpack. At this point, I was still grieving over the loss of the relationship which had ended for no valid reason and for which I absolutely needed answers to begin the process of my own healing. The title of this email was "Closure," and this was my way of asking for it. Outside of here, she actually did agree to meet me out at one of our favorite breweries to discuss closure, but it ended with her screaming at me that "None of that is any of my business anymore," as she drove off in a huff.

"Forward only" was another catchphrase, employed after the breakup. Other narcs probably have similar go-tos in these situations because they know if you thoroughly examine the past, you just may end up doing something like writing this book. They'd rather keep you on the hook - not reeled in, but injured and in their waters, available if they so desire. They believe that you mistreated them, that there's something better than you out there, and that this is your punishment. But they also need you within arm's reach in case they find themselves in need of narcissistic supply. In which case you're easily hauled back on deck for a while and expected to flop around and gulp helplessly for their enjoyment.

I had the right idea in the third paragraph. Total indifference was the only real way to go. I just didn't know it yet.

Of course she had no interest in couple's

whatever (from not me)

therapy. If they go to therapy, they're going to find out that, you guessed it, they're not perfect. A therapist is a real danger zone. They'll only go if they're sure they can convince the therapist that they're right about everything, and that's easier to do when you're by yourself.

It is actually difficult for even the most seasoned mental health professionals to identify a narcissist one-on-one. The narcissistic individual is such an expert liar that they can defy detection. What makes them such preternatural liars?

They believe their lies. They must in order to maintain their veil of perfection. The alternative is that they are not perfect, therefore the lie *is* their reality. They internalize so much that they live in an alternate reality where they are never wrong, and lying to maintain that becomes second nature, the truth a necessary casualty even when leading to devastating personal consequences.

Therefore, a narc will never voluntarily attend couple's therapy. They may go if you have enough leverage to drag them, such as children or a court order, though.

The rest of the email is mostly me

apologizing for completely normal behavior, given the circumstances. However, due to her hypersensitivity, I felt like I needed to apologize for every little thing in the hopes that one would stick and she would come back to me. This had become a pattern over a long period of time.

Just as she was throwing reasons for the breakup against the wall, I had been tossing apologies right behind them. Some, for things I hadn't really even done wrong, but that, through gaslighting, she had convinced me I had.

In other words, she had me eating out of her hand.

She would get angry over something fairly reasonable, and I would point out that this was nothing to get angry over. I was immediately labeled the problem and the one with anger issues.

More than once I was ordered to "get out of (her) house," and I would sheepishly leave and go sit on the porch or out in my car for a few minutes until she came outside to apologize and let me back in.

In the last paragraph I wax nostalgic about a few experiences that I regarded as emotional cornerstones of our relationship, but again, I didn't know about narcs and that they are incapable of the deeper understanding necessary to appreciate such events. To her this was simply a list of activities we had done together - a list that was intended to manipulate her into taking me back.

Actually, she was right about that last part. It was intended to invoke a nostalgic emotional response, but none of it worked. None of it even had hope of working.

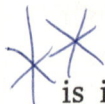

You cannot reason with a narcissist. Winning is impossible. They will lie straight to your face no matter how rational or calm you are. They will deny your victory to the point of absolute absurdity. Reality is just a suggestion when you always have to be right, and you'll be amazed at the fabrications that come from your former partner.

Now comes the part of which I am not proud.

She kept insisting on "radio silence," which didn't make any sense to me. Just as with recoiling from being kissed, this was unbelievably childish behavior. I had also been receiving mixed signals in the form of hoovering attempts and had been subjected to so much gaslighting that I wasn't sure what was real anymore.

I needed answers. We had spent almost three years together, and there had not been anything of substance wrong at all, had this been a normal relationship featuring two normal participants.

What I should have done and ultimately had to do was to extract my answers from some other source because she was never going to provide any.

The silent treatment is another common tactic used by narcs and children. They use it to punish you. They think that by limiting contact and limiting your supply of them, that it will teach you a lesson and you'll come back and apologize.

Sadly, it usually works.

I didn't know any of this yet, and I continued to attempt to coax answers out of her for entirely too long. I mistakenly still assumed her to be a normal human being who had equally valued the time that we spent by each other's sides, but with each correspondence she grew increasingly angrier until she eventually involved the law and attempted to get a restraining order against me.

I never should have taken it that far, and while I'm someone who doesn't believe in regret because all experiences ultimately lead to growth, I am ashamed that I let it get to that point. This is why you need to be careful when dealing with the narc in your life. You should under no circumstances use the word "narcissist" when dealing with them. If you really care and want them to get help, you can try illustrating to them how their behavior has affected you. Show them how their behavior has affected others as well, and outline the consequences of those actions in exquisite detail. There is no guarantee that they will be moved, however.

You simply cannot expect any kind of meaningful reception from a narcissist once you finally link all the pieces and call them out. They cannot allow the truth to escape and will embark upon a scorched-earth campaign directed at you by any means accessible to them. They want to destroy you at this point. Anyone who has figured them out is a sworn enemy. They want to ruin your name and will involve anyone and any methods available to do so. This is the sad truth of their condition, and it is why you must be very careful when exposing them. In fact, it's best not to.

As I said on the very first page, narcissism is extremely difficult to prove. The more you fight against it, the more they will simply counter and call you crazy. Any further action on your part only enforces their point, eroding your credibility and making you look . . . well, crazy to anyone involved.

It is unfortunately a zero-sum game and your only choice is to walk away.

I have found that acceptance, while difficult to obtain at first, is the best-traveled path. Remember, acceptance is about change.

What do you do with things that you cannot change? You embrace them. They are reality, so you must accept them, and if you want to be happy, you may as well accept and embrace the things you cannot change. This way, adding new things to the list - such as a death or another person's behavior - becomes easier.

This is what I do.

To illustrate, I am not a tall person. Throughout my years, I have been told more than once from friends and coworkers that they don't think of me as "short" and that they had never even registered it until they saw me standing next to someone who is tall. This is because I long ago decided that since my height was not within my control, I should just embrace it and be the best person I can be.

It took me some time to see how this philosophy can be applied to my narcissistic relationship.

It is something else over which I have no control, so it should be embraced in the same way. It is part of who I am now, and it taught me some very valuable lessons. Leaving me a better and more well-rounded person.

That is truly worth celebrating.

Before acceptance and celebration, the loss may feel overwhelming, but remember, this person put on a mask and only pretended to be your perfect partner - the unicorn that you didn't think existed.

In fact, unicorns don't exist at all. This was merely an ass in a party hat.

It can be very difficult to let go of that perceived connection, but you must remember that it was only that - perceived.

You're mourning something that was never really there. The relationship was real to you and your pain is real, but the entirety of it had been one-sided on your part. A single person cannot carry all the burden and all such relationships are doomed to failure.

You were invested in them and the relationship, but they did not and could not return the favor. They can't feel the anguish that they've caused you because they blocked that sort of pain off long, long ago. They never let you in and never became vulnerable. Without that, a true connection cannot be established.

Pay attention to past actions. Look for behavioral patterns.

Were they dismissive of your feelings? Did they often do things that didn't make sense, like take extreme offense to something that wasn't even directed at them? Did they refuse to be wrong or admit fault in any way?

Did they ever truly appreciate anything you did for them?

Was there a real lack of romance in the relationship, replaced instead by an almost clinical nature?

I am an ENFP personality type and as such, I wanted to help this woman so much that I fell for every one of her narcissistic traps, hook, line, and sinker. I have since learned to trust my instincts and have become a naval-quality spotter of red flags. I have established personal boundaries, and learned that it's okay to enforce them and to say "no."

I have become the happiest and most complete version of myself.

The practiced empath.

CLOSING
THOUGHTS

As an empathic individual, do not take their devaluation to heart. You are the rarest and most giving personality type, and that is truly a special thing.

Your only problem was that you had never encountered a dyed-in-the-wool narcissist before. You didn't know how to put up boundaries and enforce them. You wanted to help, but in the process you let the narc walk all over you. Looking back, you probably won't like how your own personality changed in order to acquiesce to the narc's demands.

In time you will learn that you are truly better off without them.

The good news is that you are still that special person who believes in truth and integrity and has a real desire to help. You will reclaim yourself and thrive, only now you're armed with the necessary tools to avoid this type of situation again. Now you know what you truly need in a relationship with another person.

Go out and find it.

It is my hope that if you picked up this book, that it has helped you gain your own closure and to grow into your full empathic potential.

Similarly, if you suspect that you yourself may have Narcissistic Personality Disorder, Kudos on picking up this little book. I hope that it has helped to illustrate the ways in which your behavior harms yourself, your loved ones, and others around you. The next step for you is to seek help in the form of a qualified mental health professional.

Made in the USA
Monee, IL
04 March 2023

29125198R00062